W9-AUN-320

MANDALAS
of the
CELTS

Klaus Holitzka

Sterling Publishing Co., Inc.
New York

3   5   7   9   10   8   6   4   2

Published by Sterling Publishing Company, Inc.
387 Park Avenue South, New York, N.Y. 10016
Originally published in Germany as *Keltische Mandalas* and
© 1996 by Schirner Verlag, Darmstadt
Distributed in Canada by Sterling Publishing
℅ Canadian Manda Group, One Atlantic Avenue, Suite 105
Toronto, Ontario, Canada M6K 3E7
Distributed in Great Britian and Europe by Cassell PLC
Wellington House, 125 Strand, London WC2R 0BB, England
Distributed in Australia by Capricorn Link (Australia) Pty Ltd.
P.O. Box 704, Windsor, NSW 2756 Australia
Printed in Mexico
All rights reserved

Sterling ISBN 0-8069-5729-8